SPARKY the Spunky Puppy

Written by Bruce Paragon
Illustrated by Ira Baykovska

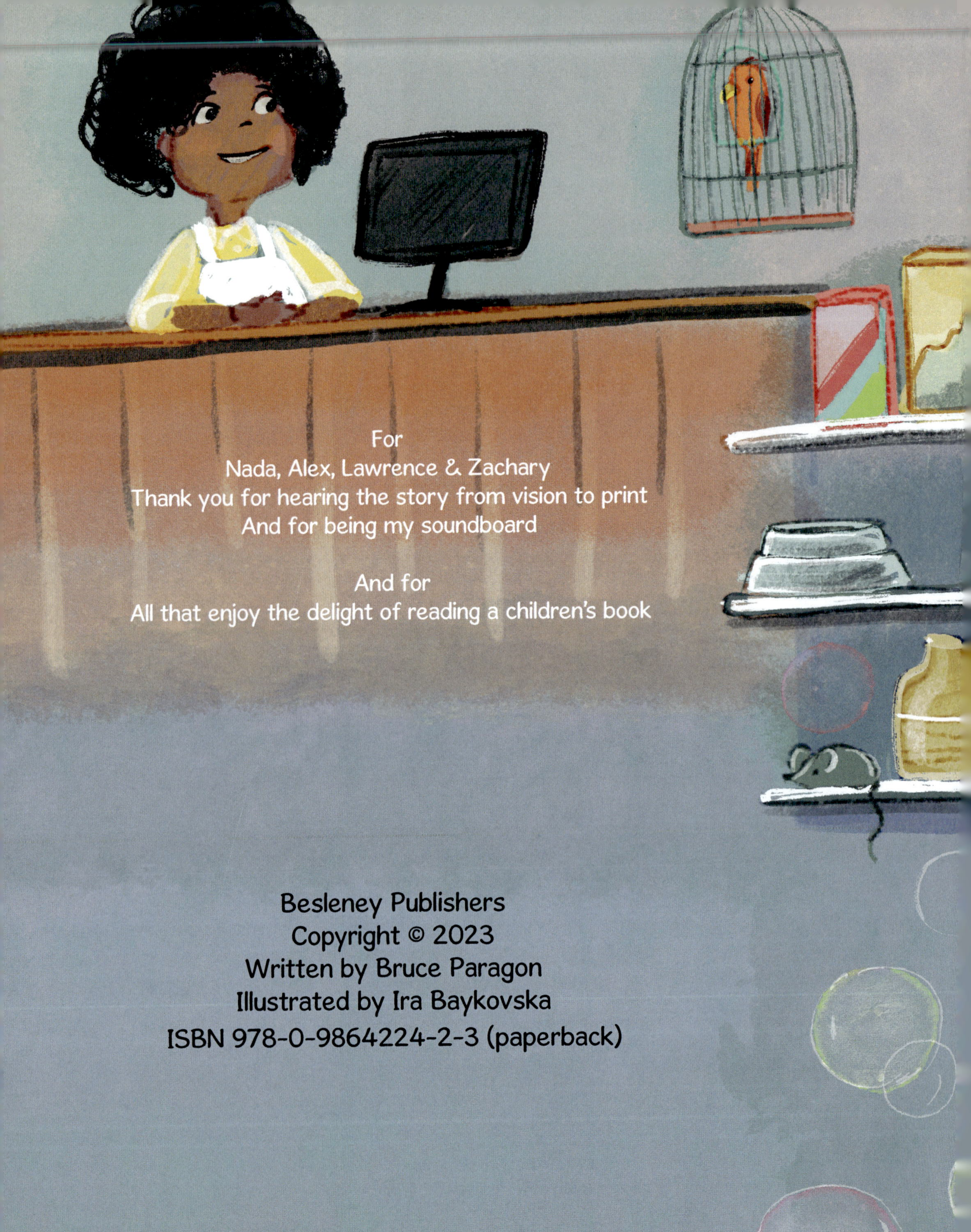

For
Nada, Alex, Lawrence & Zachary
Thank you for hearing the story from vision to print
And for being my soundboard

And for
All that enjoy the delight of reading a children's book

Besleney Publishers

Written by Bruce Paragon
Illustrated by Ira Baykovska
ISBN 978-0-9864224-2-3 (paperback)

Welcome to the pet shop. A wonderful place to be.
Full of dogs and cats and birds and Corey the bulldog - that's me.

I'm just a little older than a puppy, yes it's true.
An old dog that can learn new tricks, but has better things to do.

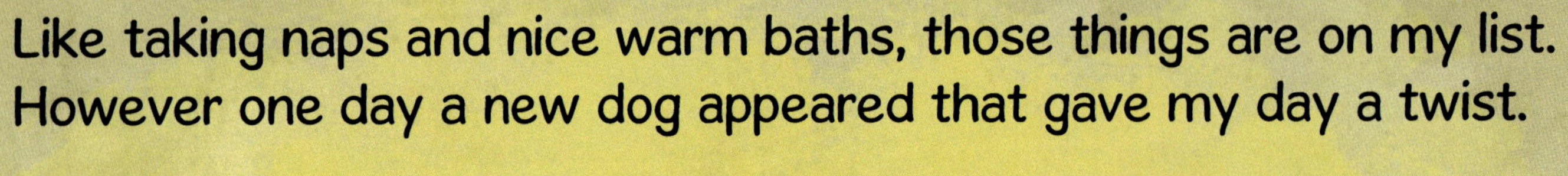

Like taking naps and nice warm baths, those things are on my list.
However one day a new dog appeared that gave my day a twist.

I like to have my bath time quiet, calm and free from noise.
So I can enjoy some bubble time with my favorite bath time toys.

Well, today that wouldn't happen. No, today was something new
A visit from a spunky pup would make this brown dog blue.

He was teeny tiny with curly fur and a sparkle in his eye.
As soon as he walked in the shop I sighed and thought,
"Oh why?"

Why today and why this shop? Why can't he go away?
But it was clear our little friend was definitely here to stay.

He walked in with a spunky bounce and swung his curly hair.
He danced right over to the tub as if floating on air.

"Hello my friend, I'm Sparky. Can I get a trim from you?
I have a party later today and need a new hairdo."

The owner nodded, "Yes indeed. Once Corey is all done."
"Thank you Ms., I'll wait right here and have a little fun."

I couldn't help but wonder what this pup was going to do.
What happened next was certainly different
and loud and spunky and new.

Sparky tossed his curly locks
that covered up one eye.
He shook his hips and moved
his feet and jumped up really high.

He danced around the pet shop,
he boogied and he twirled.
Like he was the only one in
there, the only dog in the world.

He didn't care who saw him, he danced without a care.
It was like the entire pet shop wasn't even there.

But every older dog and cat stared with big, wide eyes.
"What is going on in here?" "Who is this little guy?"

First by the door was a St. Bernard. That was my friend Marty.
A guard dog who was always prepared, but didn't like a party.

Then there was little Ms. Abbey, a kind black cat, it's true.
But she liked things a little slower and not so loud and new.

Marianna, yes, was next in line, a beautiful orange bird.
Although her feathers were wild and bright,
a calm day was much preferred.

Karl the German Shepard had a heart of gold we know.
But he always acted rough and tough and couldn't let it show.

Sparky just kept right on dancing
with a light and open heart.
Then he waltzed right by a dog
who liked him from the start.

Valentina was a Chihuahua and she was younger too.
She liked to dance and jump around. It's what she loved to do.

Sparky smiled at Valentina and then they danced together. Because dancing and laughing with a friend is always so much better.

Then suddenly something happened, to the older pet shop friends.
Something that made them smile and made them want to pretend.

Pretend that they were younger and didn't have a care.
When they had dancing puppy feet and seemed to float on air.

They all began to smile as they
watched the two pups prance.
Then up they leapt and twirled
around and all began to dance.

It was one big party and everyone joined the crew.
And danced like they were young and the world was all brand new.

I couldn't hold back either and I jumped out of the tub.
There'll always be another time for a quiet, bath time scrub.

But that day was for dancing, for being young and bold.
And that day was the first day I did not feel so old.

“Sparky, let me thank you for helping me to see.
That you are really just as old as you tell yourself to be.”

Sparky smiled as he jumped up into the grooming chair.
Ready for a little comb and a new cut for his hair.

"I could not be happier, that I helped you to know.
That as we all get older we learn lots and we grow."

"But when that happens please don't think, it means you must slow down. There's always time to dance with friends and run all over town."

Even though he was just a pup,
Sparky knew a lot.
He shared his brilliant wisdom.
He spoke right from the heart.

That day I learned some patience and always to be kind.
Those were two great lessons that I was happy to find.

Next Sparky got his hair trimmed and then unlike before.
Two eyes stared right back at me, not covered anymore.

They gleamed so bright and sparkled and they seemed to say.
"You're only as young as you feel, so let's feel young today."

He danced around just one more time and joy it filled the shop.
We all had such a wonderful time, we didn't want to stop.

But Sparky had to leave that day, so he headed for the door.
Said he'd be back to play and laugh and of course we'd dance some more.

And then in just an instant, in the quickest little blink.
He turned right back to look at me and I gave him a wink.

As a little thank you, for helping this old dog to see.
That you are truly only as old as you want yourself to be.

About the Author

Bruce Paragon grew up in northern New Jersey but now resides in Central Florida with his wife and three wonderful sons. He graduated from William Paterson University with a degree in political science before receiving his certified public management certification from Rutgers University. He spent his career in public service, ultimately retiring as a senior administrator from one of the largest law enforcement Agencies in the state.

Paragon's favorite books were science fiction and fantasy adventures as a child. He loved to delve into the works of authors such as J. R. R. Tolkien, C. S. Lewis, Isaac Asimov, J. K. Rowling, and Stephen King. Also, Paragon enjoys reading, drawing, and writing. And he loves that picture books encompass all of these things.

After starting a family, he felt compelled to write a Children's Picture Book. He draws inspiration from his wife and children. This is his debut Children's book.

About the Illustrator

Ira Baykovska is a children's book illustrator and a mom of two beautiful girls.

Ira has been drawing for as long as she can remember and sometimes cannot believe that this hobby has become her life-long career.

She has been working as a freelance illustrator since 2014 and has illustrated more than 20 books for kids. Ira has a degree in Graphic Design and currently lives and works in Lviv, Ukraine.

Visit Ira's website **www.baykovska.com**